MY PARENTS ARE DIVORCED, TOO

A Book for Kids by Kids

by

Melanie, Annie, and Steven Ford

as told to

Jan Blackstone-Ford

Magination Press • Washington, DC

This book is dedicated to
Sharyl and Jeff Walker and Jennifer and Michael Mew,
the other half of our blended family

Library of Congress Cataloging-in-Publication Data

Ford, Melanie.
    My parents are divorced, too : a book for kids by kids / by
Melanie, Annie, and Steven Ford, as told to Jan Blackstone-Ford.
      p. cm.
    Includes bibliographical references.
    Summary: Three stepsiblings in a blended family discuss their
experiences and those of friends with divorce and remarriage.
    ISBN 1-55798-450-6
    1. Children of divorced parents—Juvenile literature. 2. Divorce—
Juvenile literature. 3. Remarriage—Juvenile literature.
4. Stepfamilies—Juvenile literature. [1. Divorce. 2. Remarriage.
3. Stepfamilies.] I. Ford, Annie. II. Ford, Steven.
III. Blackstone-Ford, Jan. IV. Title.
HQ777.5.F67 1997
306.874—dc21   96-46699
                                                  CIP
                                                  AC

Published by
MAGINATION PRESS
An Educational Publishing Foundation Book
American Psychological Association
750 First Street, NE
Washington, DC 20002

Manufactured in the United States of America

10 9 8 7 6 5 4 3 2 1

Table of Contents

v

Melanie, Jan, Annie
and Steven Ford

Introduction for Parents

We often talk about a "successful" marriage, but very rarely do we hear about a "successful" divorce. With over half the marriages in the United States currently ending in divorce, we, as parents, know that our children are often the ones to suffer the most at the dissolution of a marriage. My goal through my divorce and remarriage was to make the transition as painless as possible for my kids. I quickly realized there were no guidelines or rules that could ensure everyone would be happy. Although I am blessed with very accepting "bonus children," and my husband's ex-wife and my ex-husband are extremely supportive, we found that the adjustments after remarriage are not easy ones. We learned that we had to create a lifestyle that worked for us. Through determination and love, we have broken through the stereotypical relationships many people think you must have in a stepfamily, to make a working blended family with hopefully healthy and well-adjusted children.

I would like to explain how this book came to be. The authors of *My Parents Are Divorced, Too* are Melanie, Annie, and Steven Ford. They are not all biologically related. They are what is commonly referred to as stepsiblings, children who now live together in a blended household.

One morning I was making breakfast for the kids and their friends. It was a typical Saturday morning at our house: noisy and chaotic. All of a sudden one of the friends began to cry—we thought for no reason. After much prodding, she explained that her father and mother were now separated. This was to be her weekend with her dad, but rather than be with her, he was water-skiing with his new girlfriend. She was feeling neglected and alone.

I recognized these feelings because my own "bonus daughter," Melanie, had a similar problem when her father and mother separated. I suggested Melanie give her friend a few tips on how she handled that same situation. As Melanie began to talk, her friend's tears subsided. They began to really discuss what bothered them about divorce and how to handle it. Here was living proof that children open up more freely to their friends than to adults. Within 15 minutes, Melanie's friend was again laughing and anxious to try Melanie's suggestions.

My Parents Are Divorced, Too discusses the problems Melanie, Annie, and Steven felt were the hardest to overcome when divorce was new to them. They tell you about the problems they faced and the problems their friends have discussed with them. They talk about what they did to solve their problems and what they suggested to their friends. Through their discussions, you and your children can learn how they survived divorce and contributed to the success of a blended family.

Besides being the mom of this blended family, I teach elementary school and often work with children of divorce. I also write a column for *Working Mother* magazine on stepparenting and blended family living. To write this book, I tape-recorded hours of discussions with Melanie, Annie, and Steven. Because the kids knew their conversations were being taped, they were very serious. They often forgot I was their mother during the interviews and told me things they had never discussed before. Many things had been bothering them for a long time.

If your family has gone through a divorce recently, and you are having trouble getting adjusted to your new life, the kids wrote this book for you. *My Parents Are Divorced, Too* is a survival guide for kids by kids who have been through it. Melanie, Annie, and Steven Ford understand how it feels when a divorce turns your life upside down.

My Parents Are Divorced, Too was written to help your children understand their experiences and feelings during the different stages of divorce. It can also help you to understand what your children may be feeling. It is a good book to read along with your children. Our hope is that it will serve as a vehicle to start a dialogue of open communication at a very difficult time in everyone's life.

Jan Blackstone-Ford

Introduction for Kids

Why We Wrote This Book

Our names are Melanie, Annie, and Steven. Our last name is Ford. Annie's last name is not really Ford, but when everyone in the family used the same last name except her, she felt out of place and decided to change it.

This book is a project we have worked on for a long time. We wrote it because we have already gone through our parents' divorce, so we know about some of the things that may be bothering you. We know that divorce can really hurt. And we want to help.

This book is divided into sections about different subjects, so you don't have to read the entire book if you don't want to. You can just look for the subject that interests you.

Everything we have mentioned in this book is true. We only changed some of our friends' names, so they won't get embarrassed. All of the stuff you will be reading really happened to our family.

We hope that what we talk about will help you with what is happening in your life.

You can make it! We did.

Melanie Ford
Annie Ford
Steven Ford

❖ 1 ❖

BEFORE THE DIVORCE

PARENTS' FIGHTING

Why do I feel sick when my parents fight?

Melanie: When my parents fought a lot, I would get stomachaches that were really bad. I would try to go to school, but they would send me home because my stomach hurt. My mom finally took me to the doctor because I had so many stomachaches. They couldn't find anything wrong with me. Nobody knew it was because my parents were fighting. Even I didn't know.

Q: Why didn't anyone know?

Melanie: My parents didn't think I heard them fight. I remember they would go in the bathroom and just yell at each other really loud. Their bed was right outside the bathroom. I would sit on their bed and listen to them fight. I was only four, and it

My stomach hurts.

1

Why do I feel sick when my parents fight?

really scared me. I didn't tell them I knew because I was afraid to.

What can I do about my parents' fighting?

Melanie: Try and talk to your parents and tell them how you feel. Tell them you don't like the fighting.

Annie: I didn't like it when my parents fought. I was always afraid my dad would get mad at me if I said anything. He has a real low voice and it scares me.

Steven: You have to talk to them!

Annie: Parents always think you're so dumb and just a little kid, even if you are older. They think you don't understand what is going on, and they keep things from you. Kids know. You can feel it. Even if parents aren't fighting in front of you, you can tell when they don't like each other.

Now I would say, "Hey, look, I hate it when you fight. It makes ME feel real BAD!"

Melanie: It's hard to talk to your parents when you think they may get mad at you. But what's the worst thing that could happen? Divorce? Things can't get any worse than that. Your parents' being mad at you only lasts a little while. So I would just ask them, "What's going on?"

LEARNING ABOUT THE DIVORCE

Why doesn't anyone tell me what's happening?

Melanie: I know my parents must have told me they were getting a divorce, but I didn't get it. I know I was only four, but I feel that they should have made me understand. I have asked my dad about it, and he said that my mom explained everything to me. But even if I said I understood, I didn't. I had a lot of problems dealing with it.

Steven: I was only two. I don't think anyone explained anything to me because I was so little.

Annie: My mom and dad were divorced when I was only a baby, so I never really lived with them together. My mom got married again when I was three. When I was six, my mom and my stepdad got a divorce. My mom explained everything to me, so I understood.

But I had a stepsister, Veronica, when my mom was married to my stepdad, and he didn't tell her anything when we left. She was five years older than me. I was very close to her. She told me that after we left, she went to her dad's house expecting to see my mom and me, and we were just gone. All her dad told her was that we had moved out and they were getting a divorce. Nothing more! And she was 12! She wasn't young like Steven. She was definitely old enough to understand! I guess her dad told my mom he wanted to take care of telling her what happened, and he never did.

She was still so mad at her dad that she was shaking when she told me the story. I told her she had to tell her dad how mad she was. She said she was afraid to talk to him, and she didn't think he would listen to her, anyway. She felt he really didn't care how things looked to her. It bothered her for a really long time. It made her not like her dad that much.

How can I find out what's going on?

Annie: Talk to someone who knows what really happened. Veronica decided to ask her mother. She hoped her mom would know and clear up the mystery. As things turned out, her mother did know what happened and told her where we were. But Veronica was very mad at her dad because she felt it was his place to explain why we left. When she finally came to visit us, my mom talked to her for a long time. I remember my mom felt really bad because she thought the reason Veronica hadn't called us was because she was mad at us. But it took Veronica a year to get up enough courage to ask her dad where we were. When she finally did talk to her dad about it, do you know what he said? He didn't think it was that important to her! You always think grown-ups know better, you know?

4

TAKING BLAME

Is the divorce my fault?

Annie: I felt it was my fault my mom and stepfather got a divorce. I don't even know why; I just did. I thought the fighting was my fault. My mom told me that parents want the divorce from each other, not from their kids. So that made me feel better. But you still feel very bad.

Melanie: I think kids blame themselves because they don't really understand what's happening. Either parents don't tell you exactly what's happening, or they think we are too young to understand, so they leave a lot of things out that should be explained. Both are wrong. They should just come out and tell you.

He thought it was all his fault.

Steven: One day I was playing with a friend, and he told me he was afraid his parents were going to get a divorce. He thought maybe if he was good and didn't make his parents mad, they might not get the divorce. He thought it was all his fault. I told him it wasn't, but he still felt bad. He thought his parents fought because he was bad. He blamed himself.

Melanie: I never thought that. I just didn't want it to happen.

LOYALTIES

Do I have to choose between my mom and dad?

Steven: I remember a time when my parents were fighting. They were already divorced. I was around four or five. My mom wanted to do something she knew would make my dad mad, so she told us not to tell him. Even though I was little, I knew that was wrong. I felt awful.

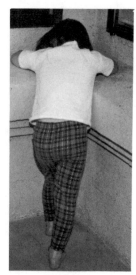

Melanie: You love BOTH your parents. That put us right in the middle, and then we felt like we had to choose which one we liked best. If we like mom best, we keep the secret. If we like dad best, we tell him the secret. It was a terrible time.

Steven: I was very upset, and I had a hard time keeping the secret. Then

I felt awful.

6

It was one of the worst of times.

one day I slipped and told our stepmom about the problem. I was glad I told. She called my mom, and they worked it out. I don't even remember what the problem was now. I just know how bad it made me feel to have to keep the secret from my dad.

Melanie: The next time I saw my mom, I told her how bad she made me feel when she asked us to keep something from my dad. My mom said she would never do that again. She didn't realize she was asking us to lie. I hated having to choose between my mom and dad. It was one of the worst times.

7

TALKING THINGS OVER

What do I do when I feel bad?

Annie: If you hold everything inside, then you act mad at everyone and treat people mean. They won't want to be around you. You just feel bad all the time. Sometimes it goes away, but it always comes back. If you talk about your problems with someone who can help you, things stop bothering you.

Steven: Sometimes I feel bad, but I don't know what to say.

Annie: You just talk about how you *feel*. The words will come.

You just talk about how you feel.

8

Steven: Annie used to seem angry a lot of the time.

Annie: Because I *was!* I am learning to talk about what bothers me. I'm much better than I used to be. I don't like to feel angry inside. Now I tell people when I am upset, and I don't feel as angry all the time. Talking about how I feel is something I had to learn. It doesn't come naturally. It does with Melanie. She has no problem opening up and telling people why she feels bad. With me it is very, very hard.

How do I even know what's wrong?

Annie: Lots of my friends have talked to me about being afraid that their parents were going to get a divorce. What I see is that most of the time the parents are so upset they don't see that their kids are upset, too. Sometimes you don't know what is wrong, so when a parent asks what's wrong, you just say nothing, because you don't know. Then the parents think everything is just fine, and it's not.

Steven: Then you get in trouble because you are so mad, and you are just doing stuff because you don't know why. Like my friend James—he's always getting into trouble.

Annie: His dad just moved out, too. I bet he feels real angry.

Melanie: When my friends talk to me about this kind of stuff, I tell them that I know how they feel because I felt those things, too. I tell them that things get better with time, and that I am there for them if they want to talk. For me, talking is what made the difference. Now look at me! Things were very bad before. Now I am just fine.

He's always getting into trouble.

GETTING HELP

Who can I talk to?

Melanie: At our school, we have a counselor who can help. You can request to see her anytime you want to talk to someone about a problem. We also have a special group called the Friendship Group. It is a group of kids who discuss their problems together with the help of the counselor. After I went, I learned that my problems were not that bad. I had parents who were getting a divorce, and that was terrible, but some of my friends had really BIG problems. My parents weren't threatening or hurting me.

Annie: When my best friend told me that her stepdad was hitting her mother, I was very upset. We were swimming, and she just started to cry for no reason. She was afraid to tell anyone because she thought her stepfather might hurt her if she told. She was very confused, and it took us a long time to decide what to do. We decided to ask my mom for help. After we talked to my mom, she called my friend's mom and talked to her. They decided my friend would stay with us for a few days while her parents worked it out. Her parents decided to get a divorce.

Melanie: If you are being hurt you have to tell somebody. There is always someone you can tell. If you're embarrassed to tell a friend, then tell your teacher or a counselor or your aunt or uncle. Just tell someone. If you feel afraid, it is a sign you need help.

The Friendship Group.

❖ 2 ❖

GOING THROUGH THE DIVORCE

HAVING TO MOVE

Why do I have to move?

Melanie: I didn't understand why I had to leave my house and my room. Even though we moved only a mile away, I still had to leave my room and my dad. My parents were the ones getting the divorce, not me. Why did I have to leave? I didn't understand that when your parents get a divorce, so do you. I didn't understand why my dad wasn't coming with us. I knew they were getting a divorce. I didn't get what "divorce" meant. I hated the whole thing.

Annie: My mom and I moved two hours away from our old home. It was a lot different from where I used to live. I liked it much better. See, we moved away from my stepfather. I didn't like him that much, so I wasn't sad to go. I felt like I could start all over. I missed my old friends, but I made new friends real fast.

Steven: I was so young I don't remember moving out.

Annie: Moving doesn't have to be that bad. At first, I didn't want to move. My mom asked me to give it a chance, and then see how I felt. I did give it a chance, and I liked it much better. That's what I would tell my friend to do. If you really don't like it, then you have to tell your mom or dad, and maybe they can change something. I mean, they probably won't live together again, but maybe they could help you like the place better. Maybe they can take you out to see what there is to do in the new town.

Melanie: When my friend Jill moved here after her parents got a divorce, she liked her old home better. She talked about it all the time. Now she is used to it here, but it has been two years.

Will I lose my old friends?

Annie: I made my old friends into pen pals. I love to get mail! We write back and forth all the time. It's fun because

Moving doesn't have to be that bad.

My old friends come to visit.

I never used to get letters, and now I do. My old friends come to visit me in the summer. It has been a long time, and we still write, and they always come to stay with me for a few days. Sometimes even their mom comes. We all have a great time.

CHANGING HOUSES

Where do I live, and when?

Melanie: We live in a very small town. When my parents first separated, my mom, Steven, and I moved just a mile away from my dad. In the beginning, we switched back and forth every other day. That was hard because I kept having to pack up every day to go to the other place, and it was very confusing. When I was in the third grade, I sometimes left my homework at the other house. I fell behind in school. Then when my dad got married again, we decided to switch houses every other week. I like that better because I still see both my parents, but now I know where I will be. We switch on Fridays. I have a room at both houses. All the parents get along, so if I want to see the other parent, I just ask and go. The biggest problem used to be that I missed my mom when I was at my dad's, and I missed my dad when I was at my mom's.

Steven: I have a friend, Sam, whose parents got a divorce. He had to live with his father, who lived two hours away, and his brother had to live with his mother. That was very bad. He missed his brother *and* his mom. Sometimes he was glad his brother lived somewhere else because then he couldn't beat him up! But he still missed him. Now his father has moved back to our town, so Sam lives with his

I left my homework at the other house.

mom and his brother, and they can see their father anytime they want. It was just too hard the other way. He likes it better now.

Annie: Lots of my friends' parents are divorced. Some live with just their mom. One lives with just his dad. I have a friend who lives with his grandparents. I have two other friends who live with both their mom and their dad, like Melanie and Steven do—one week at mom's, and the other week at dad's. I live with my mom and Larry most of the time. I see my dad every other weekend.

I wish I were somewhere else!

Melanie: I'm not sure you are ever happy all the way with where you live after a divorce. Things happen and you wish you were at the other house. Like when we go to my mom's for the weekend, and my dad goes to a baseball game, or something else I'd like to do. But I have to stay at my mom's because we haven't seen each other in a week. But sometimes we go to special places with my mom, too, so I guess it all evens itself out. It takes a while, but you get used to it.

MISSING A PARENT

Why doesn't my mom or dad spend more time with me?

Melanie: Right after my mom and dad got a divorce, I used to see my dad way more than my mom because she went

When I miss my mom, I just call her.

back to work. She never worked that much before. When I would go to my mom's house, she always had friends over or she would be on the phone and she wouldn't be with me. Then she got a new boyfriend, and he was always there. I felt very bad because I wanted to be with my mom, and I felt like people were always around. Everytime I tried to cuddle with her, my little brother would come over and bug us.

Q: What did you do?

Melanie: I talked to my "bonus mom" about it. That's what we call Jan. We don't call her our "stepmom." I talked to her, and she told me to tell my mom exactly how I felt. So I sat down with my mom, and I told her I didn't see her enough. I told her I felt like there were people around all the time. We were never together, just us. My mom said she didn't realize I felt that way and she would spend more time with us. She gave me pictures I put up in my room at my dad's house that reminded me of the good times we have had together. That way you feel like everyone is around you all the time. She also gave me a card I read every time I miss her. It tells me how much she loves me. I still have it!

Annie: When I was very little, my mom traveled on business and I stayed home with my stepdad. I would cry because I missed her, and it made it worse when I talked to her on the phone, because I wanted to be with her. My stepdad was always working, even if we were home, so I spent a lot of the time alone in my room. My mom realized it was a big problem and decided to change jobs. Now she's home all the time. Plus, she got married again, and now I have Melanie and Steven to play with and a new "bonus dad" who loves me. It's much better!

What can I do when I miss my mom or dad?

Annie: Now, when I miss my mom when I'm at my dad's house, I just call her. It used to make my dad mad if I talked to my mom when I was at his house. He said she was invading his privacy when she called. I think he was just mad that I missed my mom so much. He thought I wanted to be with her more than I wanted to be with him. I wanted to be with him, but I was used to being with my mom, and it was hard not to see or talk to her. Now he doesn't care, but in the beginning it was hard. I think he just felt left out.

Steven: I tell my friends to tell their parents when they feel bad. When I missed my mom and I was at my dad's house, I would tell my "bonus mom." We would call my mom on the phone. If she wasn't home, we would color pictures that I could give my mom or I would write her a letter. I was really little, so I couldn't write, but I would pretend, or Jan would write the words for me. That's what I would tell my friend to do. It made me feel much better.

I would write her a letter.

19

Melanie: My friend Kaitlyn has the exact same problem with her mom as I did when my parents first got a divorce. She feels very bad because her mom is always with her boyfriend. She has no private time with just her. When she talked to her mom about it, her mom said that she was very close to her boyfriend and wanted to be with him. I felt bad for Kaitlyn because she wanted her mom to make special time for her, and her mom didn't do anything. And you know what else? Now her dad has a new girlfriend, too, and Kaitlyn really feels very alone and left out.

Q: What should she do?

Melanie: I feel really bad for her. She has to figure out some way to make her parents see how bad she feels. You know what I think I'll do? Her dad is really good friends with my dad. I think I will tell my dad to talk to her dad. Then he can ask her how she feels and maybe she will talk to him.

Q: Why hasn't she said anything to her dad?

Melanie: She's not used to talking to her dad. She usually just talks to her mom. But when you are alone with your dad a lot, and not with your mom anymore, you have to learn to talk to your dad, too. You have to learn to talk to your dad all by yourself and not depend on your mom to tell him how you feel.

WISHFUL THINKING

Will my parents get back together?

Annie: Your parents are the ones getting a divorce because they want one. Most kids don't want to get a divorce, no

It was just wishful thinking.

matter how bad it gets at home. They have to do what their parents want. I always thought my parents would get back together. I thought that even when my mom got married again.

Melanie: Me, too. I used to talk about it with my "bonus mom," Jan. I remember one time when I was nine, I talked to her about it. She was married to my dad and everything. I asked her if she thought my dad and mom would ever get back together!

Annie: I really believed my parents would get back together, but I don't know why. I was little. Even when my mom was married to someone else, I still thought they might get back together.

Melanie: I know it was just wishful thinking by me. Inside I knew my parents would never get married again. They were much happier after the divorce. I just missed my

21

"family." I liked my mom and dad and brother all living in one place, and it wasn't like that anymore. That made me very sad.

Annie: I know my parents are happier the way it is now. I am happy, too. It's just sometimes I wish they weren't divorced.

Melanie and Steven: Yeah.

Melanie: No matter how long your parents are divorced, you sort of wish they would get back together.

WHEN PARENTS DATE

What if I hate my mom's or dad's date?

Steven: When you don't like your mom's or dad's friend, you have to talk to your parents and tell them how you feel.

Melanie: Kaitlyn hates her mom's boyfriend because her mom is never with her anymore. She liked him in the beginning, but now she feels her mother would rather be with him than her. When she said something to her mom, it didn't seem to matter, either.

Annie: My best friend Kelly's stepfather told her that he would like her better if she were a boy! He went fishing and she wanted to go, but he wouldn't take her because she was a girl. When he came home with a lot of fish, she felt left out and sad. He told her he would have taken her if she were a boy. He was serious. He wasn't teasing. She's hated him since then because he made her feel bad about herself. She is a girl. She'll always be a girl. How mean!

She is a girl. She'll always be a girl.

Q: Why do so many kids dislike the new people their parents date?

Melanie: Lots of reasons. Because they think their parents like their new boyfriends or girlfriends more than they like the kids. Because the new person is mean to them. Sometimes it is because you're not used to being divorced and you won't like *anyone* else. You may just hate the thought of your mom or dad with someone new.

THE WORST THINGS ABOUT
DIVORCE

Why don't people understand?

Melanie: My mom took us to the taping of one of my favorite TV shows, and they asked for families in the audience to be volunteers. They said you had to have a mom and a dad to be on the show. Because my parents are divorced, my dad wasn't with us and they picked the family behind us. It made me feel just like I used to when my parents first got a divorce. I didn't like the feeling at all.

I also remember one time my mom and stepdad went to Chicago to visit his parents, my new grandparents. They live in a beautiful place with a lake and lots of kids. I was talking about my stepdad, Jeff, to a bunch of the kids, and they started to tease me because I called my dad by his first name. I tried to explain to them that he was my stepdad, so I called him Jeff. They made me feel like I was weird because my parents were divorced. I got really embarrassed. I guess not many people where they live were divorced, so it seemed strange to them, but where I live lots of people are divorced. They didn't understand that. They just made fun of me.

Why can't we all be together for holidays?

Annie: I hate splitting holidays. It is terrible. I hate spending Christmas Eve at one parent's house and Christmas

I hate splitting holidays.

Day at the other's. I would like to see both of my parents on every Christmas, and Melanie and Steven, too! I would like us all to be together. I don't want to change anything, really. I just hate splitting holidays. It's another time when you have to pick where you want to be, and I want to be in both places!

Steven: Just getting the divorce is bad, but especially around the holidays.

Melanie: When Annie spends the holidays with her dad, it feels weird. I know she should spend time with her dad, but now I think of her as my sister, and if she's not around on the holidays, it feels like something is missing.

Annie: Yeah.

THE BEST THINGS ABOUT DIVORCE

What's good about divorce?

Melanie: You don't have to listen to your parents fight anymore. My parents get along much better now, and they are both much happier. I have two really great families!

Steven: You get double presents!

Melanie and Annie: Steven!

You get double presents!

❖ 3 ❖

NEW FAMILIES

GETTING MARRIED AGAIN

How can I get used to my new stepfamily?

Melanie: When my dad and Jan got married, I was eight, Annie was seven, and Steven was four. Our families decided together to get married. We talked about it and decided on the date, New Year's Eve. It was a new year, and we were starting over in a new "blended family." We all

Starting over in a new blended family.

got wedding rings at the ceremony. We know we are very lucky to love each other. When I go to Friendship Group and hear some of the terrible stories, I know how lucky I am. We fight, but not any more than my friends who have brothers and sisters. It has not always been this easy. We all had to make adjustments.

Annie: Looking back at the beginning, it doesn't seem that bad now, but I remember we had some big problems. I never had any brothers and sisters. It was always just me and my mom. We spent a lot of time together. Now she was spending a lot of time with me, but with Melanie and Steven, too, and I wanted her all to myself. When Melanie or Steven were sitting on her lap, I would sit right on them. This made Melanie very mad at me, because my mom couldn't have all three of us sitting on her lap, and someone would have to get up. Since Melanie was the biggest, it was always Melanie. She felt left out.

Melanie: I was always very mad at Annie. She moved to my home and moved into my room. She was taking all my friends. She dressed the same way I did. She never let me be with Jana. We were all trying to get to know each other and it was a hard time. Finally we decided that when Steven and I went to see our mom, it would be a good time for Annie to be just with her mom, too. But now we all blend together. A lot of times Annie comes with me when I go see my mom. They like each other very much. It was just very new in the beginning.

Annie: We went to counseling, too, Mel. Remember when you drew those pictures of me and then crumpled them up?

28

I was always very mad at Annie.

Melanie: That's right! We went to see Brenda, a counselor we go to sometimes. I told her how mad I was at Annie. She helped me get my anger out by using my words and drawing pictures. I drew pictures of Annie, and then I crumpled them up because I was mad at her. Then Annie came in and we drew pictures together. She started crumpling pictures up, too. I think she was just mad at me for crumpling up pictures of her! I can't remember much more. That was a long time ago.

What do I call my stepparents?

Melanie: When my mom married Jeff, I didn't like to call him my stepdad because some of my friends don't like their stepparents, and it just sounds weird to me. I told my mom

29

We like each other now.

and she said she understood. One day she and Jana were watching one of my basketball games, and they were discussing what to call the stepparents. One of my friends' parents joked and said to call them "bonus parents." We thought that was cool because when you get a bonus it's something good, not bad. So now we call the stepparents "bonus parents." It started out as a joke.

Steven: When I was three, my dad got married again. Then I had two moms. I can't remember not having two moms.

The only bad thing I remember is my mom didn't like me calling my bonus mom "Mom." She told me it made her feel very bad.

Q: How did that make you feel?

Steven: Like I was doing something wrong or something. I didn't know what to do. I decided to tell my bonus mom I couldn't call her "Mom" anymore. I didn't want to make my mom feel bad. It was hard to get used to because I'm with my bonus mom a lot, and I love her. When I would slip and call her "Mom," I would feel very bad. So we decided to make up a special name for her. Her real name is Jan, and I call her "Jana." Now Melanie calls her "Jana," too. She likes it because it's her special name, and my mom likes it because I call just her "Mom." It didn't make that much difference to me. I didn't see what the big deal was.

GETTING ALONG

How can I get along with my new family?

Annie: You have to figure out what your goal is. Is it to get along or not? If it is to get along, then try to be nice. Try not to get jealous. That was very hard for me. I was afraid I wasn't special to my mom anymore. My mom explained to me that I was very special, and I was the only Annie she was ever going to have. That made me feel much better.

Melanie: At the beginning, it is all very new. No one really knows each other that well, so you have to try to cooperate and help each other get to know one another.

31

What if I don't like my new family?

Annie: We never had that problem. We get mad at each other, but it isn't 'cause we don't like each other. Sometimes they just BUG me. Our family made a pact that we would not call ourselves a "stepfamily." We were just a "family," no "step," and Melanie and Steven were my sister and brother. Then one day one of my friends' mom introduced me as Melanie's stepsister. I hated that. I was very mad. I'm still mad! It really bugged me. We're sisters. I live with her, don't I?

Melanie: That's not what she meant, Annie.

Annie: I know, but it still made me mad. I never had a "real" sister. Then we got married and I had Melanie and Steven, and I was very excited. We all blended together. I felt like

We all blended together.

my mom's friend was trying to separate who was the "real" brother and sister, and I was left out. People are always asking who belongs to what parent. "Now, let me see," they say, "you are Jan's daughter, aren't you? And Steven and Melanie belong to Larry?" Or they say, "Annie is not your real sister, is she?" How do they think those questions make me feel?

Steven: If I didn't like my stepbrother or stepsister, I would try to figure out why.

Melanie: I have a friend who is afraid of her stepbrother. He is five years older than her, and he tried to touch her in a way she didn't like when their parents left them alone. She told me this a while ago. She told me she tried to tell her mom, but her mom didn't believe her. I can't imagine telling my mom something like that and having her not believe me! I think they finally went to counseling, but it took years. I think if kids tell their parents that something bad is happening to them, their parents should believe them.

FAMILY DISCUSSIONS

What can my new family do to get along better?

Melanie: We have Family Discussions. That's how we work out our problems. It doesn't matter what the problem is. That's how we worked out the problem with Annie and us and her being jealous.

How do Family Discussions work?

Melanie: Our Family Discussions have rules. First, anyone in the family can call a Family Discussion, and we all have to come. No one can stay in their room or say they are busy. Next, we all have listen to the one who has the problem. No one can interrupt or laugh. No one can loose their temper. Then we all try to work out the problem together. Sometimes it takes a few minutes. Sometimes it takes a long time. The last rule is that no one can leave the table until the problem is solved and everyone agrees.

Annie: It works, but Steven always laughs. When things get too serious, he starts to makes noises and tries to change the subject.

Steven: No, I listen. I like when we have Family Discussions.

Melanie: Sometimes Dad loses his temper, too, but he tries not to.

What kinds of problems can you work out?

Melanie: Lots of things. I'm 10 months older than Annie. I'm one grade higher than her. Sometimes we fight. If we don't get along, there is usually another problem we haven't talked about that is bugging us. Maybe I got into a fight at school with a friend, or Annie butts into my business. Sometimes she really BUGS me. When we get so mad we can't stand it, and we are making everyone miserable, someone calls a Family Discussion. It could be anyone in the family.

A Family Discussion.

Annie: You think you're so-o-o-o-o much older than me, Melanie. We have also called a Family Discussion when someone got bad grades, so the parents made new homework rules, and when someone wasn't doing their chores. I called a Family Discussion because I was upset with Larry when Mom had to go out of town on business. We had to wait for Mom to come home, though, because everyone has to come to the Family Discussions. Then we worked out the problem together.

Melanie: I've called a Family Discussion when my dad and Jana were working too hard and I wanted to spend more time with them. They didn't realize they weren't paying any attention to us. They were shocked when I told them. So if my friends said they hated their new family, I would suggest a Family Discussion to try to talk it out. It works

35

for us. The main thing is, you can't get mad. You have to remember it is a way to make things better.

Steven: Jana calls a Family Discussion when the feeling in the house just gets too tense. We all try to figure out what we can do to change it.

WHEN YOU DON'T GET ALONG

What if I don't like my stepmom or stepdad?

Annie: I didn't like my first stepdad. He was always mad at me. What did I do? Since I was the only kid, I spent a lot of time by myself.

Q: Did you ever talk to him about it?

Annie: I was only six years old. I was afraid to talk to him. I was afraid he would yell at me. Sometimes he acted like I wasn't there. He would do stuff that would get me in trouble. Like the time he took the little piece of chicken instead of the big piece he was supposed to take. My mom always made a little piece of chicken for me so I could finish all my dinner. I couldn't finish the big piece of chicken, and I got in trouble for not eating all my dinner. He sent me to my room. That kind of stuff made me not like him much.

Q: Wasn't that just a misunderstanding?

Annie: There were a lot of misunderstandings like that. I tried to be as good as I could. I was glad when we moved away.

Q: Did you talk to your mom about the problems with your stepdad?

Annie: Oh, I did, but then my mom would feel bad, and she would talk to my stepdad, and he would get mad, and sometimes it would start more fights.

Melanie: My friend Jessica told me she thinks her stepdad likes his own kids better than her. She never sees her dad, so she feels left out. Now she hates her stepdad. I told her to tell her mom why she is so mad at him all the time, because her mom can't figure out what is wrong.

Q: Did she?

Melanie: No, she's afraid to. Her stepdad has a very bad temper.

Steven: If she doesn't say something to her mom, it will never get better.

Melanie: My mom married Jeff about a year ago and we really like him.

Steven: But we don't always get along with Jeff. Sometimes we fight, too.

Annie: I don't always get along with Larry, either, but I don't know if that is because he is my "bonus" dad. My cousin gets along with her dad just like I get along with Larry. I think people just fight sometimes.

What can I do if my stepparent is mean to me?

Annie: I think I would say, "Mom, I have a problem, and I need to talk to you about it. It's a very bad problem, so don't get mad." Whenever I say, "Don't get mad," my mom knows I'm serious and tries not to get mad. If nothing is said, things will never change. Maybe her stepdad doesn't even know he's doing things that upset her.

Steven: Sometimes kids won't like anyone. It's not the stepparent's fault. Kids just want their parents to get back together. I think a lot of kids think their stepparent doesn't care about them or what they think.

Annie: It's pretty hard, because parents always think they are right. Most kids hate it when there's fighting. So they won't say anything when there is a problem if they think it will start a fight. I found that things just get worse when I don't talk to someone. If you really hate your stepmom or stepdad, I would say, ask your other parent for help. There may be a good reason. If the parent you ask for help doesn't listen or understand how important the problem is, tell someone else who could help.

One of my best friends, Angela, has a big problem with her stepmother. She moved away because of it. Her dad thinks it's just because she wanted to go live with her mom, but that's not it. There's a lot of stuff he doesn't know.

Angela is an African-American and so is her dad, but her stepmom is white. My friend does not get along with her stepmother at all. I don't know if it had anything to do with her stepmom being white. When her father was not around, her stepmom was really mean to her. She yelled at her and swore at her. I told her to tell her dad, but she said that her stepmom lied and said that she was lying. Then her dad would get mad at her. Her dad really had no idea how bad things were when he was at work!

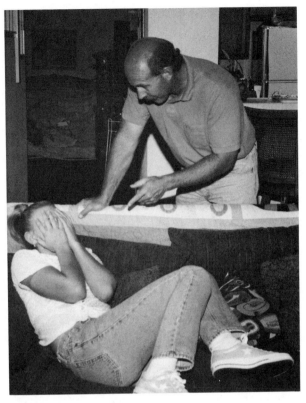

People just fight sometimes.

Angela's mom lives in Georgia. I told her to tell her mom and maybe her mom can talk to her dad, because that's what I always do. She said her mom and dad didn't get along, either. When they talk, they only fight. She felt all alone. She finally decided to go live with her mom in Georgia, just to get away. I miss her a lot. A really bad thing that happened was that she came back to visit for a month this summer, and she stayed at a friend's house. Her dad didn't even know that she was here!

Melanie: That's wrong, Annie. Her mom should have called her dad. *She* should have called her dad!

Annie: I guess her parents just don't talk to each other. She didn't want to call her dad because he would make her stay with him, and she didn't want to see her stepmom.

WHEN PEOPLE TEASE

What if friends make fun of my family?

Melanie: When Annie and I were little, we liked to dress like twins. We liked to look alike. We thought it made us "real" sisters. As we get older, we are NOT alike at all. My friends like to go to basketball games and we are into sports. Annie's friends are really different from us. They dye their hair that dark brown color and wear real baggy clothes. We listen to totally different music. At school my friends tease Annie. It really makes me mad. I have to stick up for her all the time.

Annie: Just 'cause we like different things, it doesn't mean we're really different.

Melanie: No, I know. But our styles are completely different. I know your friends tease you about me, too.

Annie: Yeah.

Steven: I hate when people tease me. It really makes me feel bad, but I just ask them how they would feel if I made fun of their sister or brother, or mom or dad. Then I just ignore them. I think you should always stick up for your family. It makes me feel bad when kids tease me, but I stick up for my family and just ignore them.

Melanie: You know what I did? I made sure that when my friends spent the night on the weekends, they got to know Annie. We all sat around and talked or watched TV. She's really funny and she makes us laugh. Then when we went to school they knew her, and now they laugh when they see each other. Now they don't make fun of her anymore. Sometimes we even hang out together.

Steven: My best friend's mom is gay. When she got a divorce from his dad, nobody told my friend or his big brother, but lots of adults knew, so other kids found out. Then kids started to tease my friend and his big brother because their mom is gay. My friend and his brother didn't know what everyone was talking about. After a while they found out it was true, and his brother told me he knew about it.

Q: Did the teasing stop?

Steven: No, it still hasn't. I don't know how it makes my friend feel. He doesn't talk about it. I know it makes his big brother feel bad. He gets very embarrassed. I don't tease my friend, though— not about that. I tease him about other stuff because we're friends, but I don't say anything about his mom being gay. All of our parents are best friends and we do lots of things to-

I feel bad when kids tease me.

41

Why do people hurt my feelings?

gether. I see them all the time. His mom is no different to me now. She's still the same person. He's still my best friend.

Melanie: Annie, do you remember when you were talking about your friend Angela, whose stepmother is white and she is African-American? Do you think their problem really is because she is black and her stepmother is white? Does she get teased about that?

Annie: Not really. Her dad is African-American. I know that if a person was nice to me, I wouldn't care what color they were, and I think she is like that, too. I would be glad they were part of my family. If my friends teased me, I would tell my friends to stop in a way that they would know I was serious. If your friends see you are serious about something, and they are really your friends, they will stop bugging you. You just have to stand up and be strong and deal with it.

Why *do people hurt my feelings?*

Melanie: I can tell you about when one of my friends really hurt my feelings. Actually, it was one of my friends' parents. They were introducing me to one of their friends, and they said I came from a "broken home." Broken home? I have *two* great homes!

Q: What would you have rather they said?

Melanie: Why did she have to say anything when she introduced me? Who cares if my mom and dad are divorced?

Annie: You know what used to make me feel really bad? When I would go to visit my dad and he would say mean things about my mom and where we live. I love my new family and where we live. It made me feel very uncomfortable. I told my mom how bad it made me feel. I didn't want to go see my dad anymore. She asked me how I wanted to handle it. We decided that we would write my dad a letter and explain how I was feeling. Then, after he got the letter, we could all discuss it. So that's what we did. When my dad got the letter, it made him think. My dad doesn't do that anymore.

FIGHTING AFTER THE DIVORCE

What if my parents keep fighting?

Melanie: You always get the same feelings when your parents fight. It doesn't matter if they are married or divorced. You don't want them to fight, ever. If friends ask me what to do, I tell them to ignore it, because it just makes you feel worse if you think about it. My parents have been divorced for eight years now, and they don't fight at all anymore. As a matter of fact, all my parents are very good friends. But in the beginning it wasn't like that, and I hated it.

A NEW BABY

Will a new baby spoil everything?

Melanie: When Jana got pregnant, on the outside we were all very excited. Everyone in the family really wanted another baby. But inside I was a little worried. Everybody told me I was going to have problems. My aunt, my mom, my other aunt, everybody would say, "Just wait until that baby is born. Things will be so different. Jana will never spend any time with you. Everything will change." I was really scared because I liked the way things were. I never said anything to anyone. Then, when Harleigh was born, we were all so happy. I have more responsibilities now, but nothing else has changed. I should have just let things go in one ear and right out the other.

Steven: I was worried, too, but I didn't say anything. I didn't like her much right after she was born. She didn't do anything. I didn't like it when she cried. Now she smiles, but not all the time.

Annie: I was very happy Harleigh was coming, but I did have one big problem. I was afraid my mom wouldn't love me as much anymore. I thought maybe because she gets along so

44

We were all so happy.

well with my bonus dad, and isn't married to my dad anymore, that she would love this baby more than she loves
me. I never said a word, though. Now I understand that
moms don't do that. I should have said something to her,
and she would have told me, but I was embarrassed. I didn't
know. We were talking one day before the baby was born,
and we realized that this baby would be just as much my
sister as Melanie's and Steven's. She joins us all together.
Then I realized how silly I had been. I never told anyone
until right now.

Melanie: I have another kind of problem with Harleigh. I
was always afraid she would like Annie more than me be-

cause Annie lives with her all the time and I had to go to my mom's house every other week. I used to worry about it all the time. Actually, the opposite happened. I feel so guilty when I leave and she cries for me! I don't know what to do. It's hard to explain to *her* about divorce. So I talk to her. I tell her I love her. I tell her she can call me anytime she wants. Sometimes Jana brings her over to visit me at my mom's house.

NEW RELATIVES

Why don't my grandparents understand?

Steven: You work hard to make your new family work, and sometimes relatives do things that split you apart. They don't even know it.

Annie: They don't understand how important it is to be a family. They knew only you before, so they forget and leave the new half out. My grandmother used to remember my birthday, but she would forget Melanie's and Steve's. She was nice to them; she would just forget their birthdays. As time went on she would remember, but on my birthday she would sneak extra money to me to buy something special.

Steven: That hurt our feelings.

Annie: My grandmother died last year, and we miss her very much, but I remember overhearing a conversation when my mom was really upset with her. It was hard to get through to my grandmother that she was doing something that was hurting our family.

Melanie: That's when you feel like a step-child.

Annie: When you start a new family, everyone you are related to has to understand what you are trying to do and support you, otherwise feelings get hurt. Like when we were little, Melanie and Steven would go to the pumpkin patch

Grandma remembered.

each year around Halloween to pick out a pumpkin to carve into a jack-o'-lantern. They would go with their Grandma Grace, their mom's mom. When I moved in, Grandma Grace just started taking me along with them. When Harleigh was born, she took Harleigh, too. I'm not really related to Grandma Grace, but she took me, and it made me like her a lot.

MAKING NEW FAMILIES WORK

What else can I do to make things work?

Annie: Try to think of everyone as one family, together. That should be your goal. Do you want this to work? If you don't, why? Because you are mad? If you are mad at each other,

47

Grandma Grace took us all to the pumpkin patch.

you will not think of each other as your family. You will think they are your enemy and you won't get along. Then no one will be happy. Not your mom, not your dad, not you.

Our family made a pact in the beginning that we would not call ourselves a stepfamily. We were just a "family," and that has always been very important to me. I also think it is important to realize that there are no set rules on how to make everyone happy after a divorce. You have to make things up as you go along.

Steven: Yeah. And if things don't work, that doesn't mean your family failed. Just try something else.

Melanie: You have to remember that you have two families now, and that is not a bad thing. Lots of times kids automatically think that things are bad and choose sides. You don't have to choose. You can love both your parents and both your families. I have a mom and she is married to Jeff. We like him very much. That is one family. And I have my dad, Jana, Annie, Steven, and Harleigh in my other family. Steven is part of both families, too. Annie has her own other family. We have lots of people who love us. No one is better than the other. And remember to talk out your problems. You are all in it together.

Steven: Just try to get along.

We are all in it together.

ACCEPTING DIFFERENCES

What if I'm different from my family?

Annie: I have something really important to add. Remember that people from different families are different from each other and don't see things the same way. This is a problem that my "bonus" dad and I are still working on, and it is very hard. He's known Melanie and Steven all their lives. They look at things differently than I do. Sometimes he gets mad at me because I don't act like they do. Like when he teases me. I hate to be teased. It really makes me mad. I hate to be tickled. Melanie and Steven love it. So if he teases me and I get mad, then he gets mad, too, and that starts a big fight.

I also like to be by myself and read. Larry, Melanie, and Steven don't really like to be by themselves. I'll be upstairs reading, and Larry will want me to come downstairs and watch TV with the rest of the family. I get mad because I don't want him to be mad at me, but I want to stay upstairs and read. You just have to remember that everyone in a blended family comes from different places, and you have to let them be themselves. You have to accept the differences.

CONCLUSION

We know the hurt feelings from a divorce don't go away for a long time. A few years have gone by since we began to write this book, and we still don't like to split holidays or be teased about being divorced. But things are definitely better, and they will get better for you, too.

If we could suggest one thing from our own experiences, we would tell you to always tell your parents how you feel. Even if you don't understand *why* you are feeling bad, tell them. This will give them a chance to help you.

We hope that reading this book has helped.

Melanie, Annie, and Steven

Resources

Organizations

National Council on Family Relations, "Focus Group" on Remarriage and
Stepfamilies, 3989 Central Avenue NE #550, Minneapolis, MN; 612-871-
9331

Stepfamily Association of America, 215 Centennial Mall South, Suite 212, Lin-
coln, NE 68508; 402-477-7837

Stepfamily Foundation of Illinois, P.O. Box 3124, Oak Park, IL 60303; 708-
848-0909

Stepfamily Foundation of New York, 333 West End Avenue, New York, NY
10023; 212-877-3244

Books for Kids

Dear Mr. Henshaw, by Beverley Cleary, 1984, Dell, 144 pages. A child writes to
an author and tells him his problems, including divorce and remarriages.
For ages 5-12.

Dinosaurs' Divorce: A Guide for Changing Families, by Laurene K. Brown and
Marc T. Brown, 1988, Little, Brown, 32 pages. A popular book for young
children.

My Mother Got Married (and Other Disasters), by Barbara Park, 1989, Alfred
A. Knopf, 128 pages. For ages 8-12.

Sam Is My Half-Brother, by Lizi Boyd, 1992, Puffin Books, 32 pages. A little
girl learns to appreciate her new brother. For ages 4-9.

What Am I Doing in a Stepfamily? by Claire Berman and Lyle Stuart, 1982,
Carol Publishing Group, 48 pages. For children who have a parent remar-
rying. For ages 5-12.

Games for Kids

Divorce Cope. Theraplay, Inc. P.O. Box 762, Monsey, NY 10952; 212-991-
1909. A board game for 2-4 to help kids and adults talk about events and
feelings related to divorce and remarriage. For ages 8-adult.

The Kids' Divorce Kit, by Ken Magid and Walt Schreibman. KM Productions, Lakewood, CO 80215; 303-969-9646. Coloring book with audio cassette. For ages 3-12.

The Kids' Stepfamily Kit, by Ken Magid and Walt Schreibman. KM Productions, Lakewood, CO 80215; 303-969-9646. Coloring book with audio cassette. For ages 3-12.

Books for Adults

How to Win as a Stepfamily, by John S. Visher and Emily B. Visher, 1991, Brunner/Mazel, 224 pages.

Putting Kids First: Walking Away from a Marriage Without Walking Over the Kids, by Michael L. Oddenina, no date given, Family Connections, 151 pages.

Step-by-Stepparenting: A Guide to Successful Living with a Blended Family, by James D. Eckler, 1993, Betterway Books, 224 pages.

Vicki Lansky's Divorce Book for Parents: Helping Your Children Cope with Divorce and Its Aftermath, by Vicki Lansky, 1996, Book Peddlers, 240 pages.

Magazines for Adults

Parenting Magazine, 301 Howard Street, San Francisco, CA 94105

Working Mother Magazine, 230 Park Avenue, New York, NY 10169

OTHER MAGINATION PRESS TITLES

ADD and the College Student: A Guide for High School ad College Students with Attention Deficit Disorder

Adolescents and ADD: Gaining the Advantage

Breathe Easy: Young People's Guide to Asthma

The Case of the Scary Divorce: A Jackson Skye Mystery

Depression Is the Pits, But I'm Getting Better: A Guide for Adolescents

Double-Dip Feelings: Stories to Help Children Understand Emotions

Gentle Willow: A Story for Children About Dying

Gran-Gran's Best Trick: A Story for Children Who Have Lost Someone They Love

I'll Know What to Do: A Kid's Guide to Natural Disasters

I Want Your Moo: A Story for Children About Self-Esteem

Into the Great Forest: A Story for Children Away from Parents for the First Time

Learning to Slow Down and Pay Attention

Little Tree: A Story for Children with Serious Medical Problems

Luna and the Big Blur: A Story for Children Who Wear Glasses

Many Ways to Learn: Young People's Guide to Learning Disabilities

Otto Learns About His Medicine: A Story About Medication for Hyperactive Children

Proud of Our Feelings

Putting on the Brakes: Young People's Guide to Understanding Attention Deficit Hyperactivity Disorder (ADHD)

The "Putting on the Brakes" Activity Book for Young People with ADHD

Russell Is Extra Special: A Book About Autism for Children

Sammy the Elephant and Mr. Camel: A Story to Help Children Overcome Bedwetting

Sammy's Mommy Has Cancer

Sarah and Puffle: A Story About Diabetes for Children

Survival Guide for College Students with ADD or LD

Tanya and the Tobo Man: A Story in English and Spanish for Children Entering Therapy

Uncle Willy's Tickles: A Story for Children About Saying No

What About Me? When Brothers and Sisters Are Sick

Wish Upon a Star: A Story for Children with a Parent Who Is Mentally Ill

You Can Call Me Willy: A Story for Children About AIDS

Zachary's New Home: A Story for Foster and Adopted Children